10-84

Karen,
from your friends at
First Presbyterian.
God bless you.
Carol Gregg

SURVIVAL PRAYERS
FOR YOUNG MOTHERS

Survival
Prayers
for
Young Mothers

By Deborah Aydt Holmes

JOHN KNOX PRESS
ATLANTA

Second Printing, 1982

Library of Congress Cataloging in Publication Data

Holmes, Deborah Aydt, 1949–
  Survival prayers for young mothers.

    1.   Mothers—Prayer-books and devotions—English.
I.   Title.
BV4847.H55   242'.6'43   76–12390
ISBN 0–8042–2195–2
© 1977 John Knox Press
Printed in the United States of America

For
Patti Underwood Aydt
and
Charles William Aydt

. . . with love beyond the telling of it

"I will increase your labour and your groaning, and in labour you shall bear children."

Genesis 3:16,
The New English Bible

Diverse children have their different natures: some are like flesh which nothing but salt will keep from putrefaction, some again like tender fruits that are best preserved with sugar. Those parents are wise that can fit their nurture according to their nature.

Anne Bradstreet (1612-1672),
"Meditations Divine and Moral"

"My daughter, your ordeal is over. . . . Holy angels will come to meet you."

Isaac Bashevis Singer,
A Crown of Feathers

PROLOGUE

In a long-distance conversation, my editor imagined he was transacting literary business when he said:

The young mothers
who pick up this book
will need to hear
that they are valued;
that they are important.
Hearing this, I think,
would be like a cool drink of water
offered in a parched desert.

His words fell like free-form poetry on my ears. I plucked them from the rest of our rather prosaic conversation and have reproduced them here, because his insight was piercingly accurate.

As a young mother, I have sometimes felt dowdy, harassed, and unappreciated. After the rigors of childbirth, my recollection is that each of my friends rushed to see the new baby—and I was left alone with my afterpains and self-pity.

Today, as I write, I am a stronger, happier woman. I feel confident and serene. I enjoy mothering, relish most of the hours I share with my children, and anticipate each coming day with something akin to excitement.

It was a long journey, however, from the moment of birth to this plateau of relative calm and certainty. There were many struggles.

I needed help. I asked for it. And I got it.

I am grateful to the following people for their encouragement in the preparation of this manuscript:

William A. Holmes, Jr.

Dona Janeway

Richard A. Ray

Paul Schumacher

Ann Underwood

The Rabbit Died

God, please help me.

I'm going to have a baby.

It should be the happiest of times. My marriage is sound. My health is good. I wanted to be a mother more than anything in the world.

Yet now that a child is actually growing within me, I wonder if I'm really ready for parenthood? Perhaps we should have postponed this baby for a while.

Perhaps we should remain childless.

People don't seem to get excited about having families any more. They get excited about freedom and careers instead. When I tell my friends about this pregnancy, I sense that their responses are cautious, even tepid.

Congratulations—if you're happy about it.

Congratulations—you're going to keep working, aren't you?

That's wonderful, a baby—that won't cramp your style too much, will it?

I don't know what I expected, God—but not this. Oh, not this.

I'm going to have a baby—and it's nothing like I thought it would be. Please lend me your strength. Let me lean on you, before a new life leans on me.

I have so much to learn in such a short time.

What You Gonna Name that Pretty Little Baby?

I can close my eyes and see the past so clearly, God.

It's Christmastime; I'm a child again.

Elementary school angels stand stiffly, stock-still, balancing shirt-cardboard "wings."

Five more minutes, and the third-grade heavenly host will be cued to march toward the holy manger.

Outside, the three wise men (chosen for height and brawn), are already singing:

> Hey, Mary! What you gonna name
> That pretty little baby?
> Glory! Glory!
> Glory to the new-born king!*

Eventually, everyone in that long-ago pageant raised his voice in song. I've forgotten if the music was flawed or irregular—it must have been, given our ages.

I remember only the beauty of the night, the haunting, plaintive melody that swelled until it filled the tiny auditorium, as names for the Christ child were weighed and discarded, then considered again . . . .

So many years ago, God.

Here I am, a woman, carrying a child of my own —considering what his name will be.

Help me to think of a strong, resonant name, God. A proud name—whatever the sex of this baby.

Thank you.

*Words from an old Negro spiritual. Author unknown.

Giving Birth

The baby was so still today, God.

The two of us are breathless with waiting.

Any time . . . somehow, a woman knows.

I could deliver today. Tomorrow. Next week. But it won't be long.

And I'm afraid. I confess it without shame—for if You can't understand and sympathize, who can?

I've anticipated the arrival of this child with such joy. The nursery is ready. My arms are impatient, an arc of emptiness, aching to hold the baby. I should be relieved that my time is drawing near.

But I'm afraid . . .

I know there will be great pain. All the mothers I know say the suffering is "worth it." But when I ask "How bad is it, really?", no one will tell me. No one will let me talk out my fears.

Is there room in your heart for a coward, God? I'm tired of hearing people say "it will be worth it." They mean well, but it's not their problem; their pain. Everyone is anticipating the coming baby—sometimes I feel no one cares about me.

Please hold my hand as we go through this together. Help me to endure the pain. Let my baby be normal, bright, and whole.

I need you as I've never needed you before, God.

Giving Birth (The Moment)

I see You through a haze of pain.

Help me, God.

The baby is bearing down, with more force than I dreamed possible.

There are lights everywhere. Metal instruments are clinking efficiently. I am surrounded by faceless people, peering down at me through gauze masks.

Help me, God.

"Push," the doctor tells me. "Push harder."

Help me, God.

"Once more," the doctor says, knitting his brows, cradling my baby's head.

Help me, God.

Light and pain are everywhere. Looking past the glare, into infinity, I sense Your warm, strong presence.

And then, soaring above the pain, above this room, I sense the presence of another . . . a tiny, lifeless body. Your spirit enters him; he breathes.

I hear an enraged, thrilling, faraway cry.

It is finished, God. At last—a perfect child.

Thank you for staying with me.

Thank you for this healthy, squalling baby.

What Do I Do Now?

"When you first touch your baby," my mother said to me, "it will be like beholding the ocean . . . you will be bathed in an indescribable love."

I'm waiting for that ocean, God.

In the past, I've grown to love people gradually, after months—sometimes years.

Mother-love is different from any other kind. There's no leisure involved, no getting-to-know. You're handed a new baby—a stranger—and a surge of affection is supposed to envelop you.

Isn't it?

Right now, at this moment, my baby and I are rather wary of each other. Love will come—it's coming already—but I really don't think it's instinctive, God.

Before we love, let us relax. Let us trust each other. Let us work through our feelings of belonging-together.

Let us celebrate all the other human emotions: yearning, need, contentment, joy.

Then we'll be ready to love—the fierce, forever sort of love that will hold our expanding family together.

Help our feelings for each other to grow and strengthen, God.

Is He Still Breathing?

God, please still the anxieties that torment me, as I listen in the night for my sleeping baby.

I know you are with him.

I know he is slumbering peacefully, normally.

Still, I can't seem to relax; to quit listening. Sleep, when it comes, is light and troubled.

His small movements, however muted, wrench me awake instantly.

A cough, a moan—however soft—send me scurrying to his crib to investigate.

You've seen the circles under my eyes, God; you've watched as I stumble, half-awake, through my daily routine.

I need rest so badly. Yet when night finally comes, and I'm on the verge of drifting off to sleep . . . I can't hear the baby breathing. So I get up to check him, and fall back into bed somehow.

God, please calm me.

Help me to remember that even the smallest of your children are sturdy enough to survive the night.

He Finally Smiled at Me

For weeks now I've been staring at this baby's inscrutable features.

Sometimes his face contorts in rage.

At other times, he sleeps or stares or does his eye-crossing trick.

This morning, though, he smiled—not a gas-bubble wince, but a real smile, God. He broke into a crooked, glorious grin, as if we were sharing a joke together. His eyes crinkled; his lips curved upward until his gums were exposed.

I laughed with joy, and I think the noise frightened him—he looked startled and serious once more, and began to cry.

So I picked him up, and held him tightly, and nuzzled against his warm, soft, lightly-fuzzed head.

This baby is beginning to turn into a person, God. He's responding to your world, and to the people who care for him.

I'm beginning to feel that ocean of love, God.

It just took a while.

The Baby-Sitter

Please keep an eye on this baby-sitter, God.

She came with references, but something about her troubles me. When she picks up the baby, she looks at him as if he were . . . just another baby.

"Don't worry, Mother," she says to me. "We'll be just fine."

I'm "mother." And I *am* worried.

This is my first trip away from him. I'm going to have an adult evening with my husband, to recapture some of the romance that went out of our marriage when the baby came in.

I've looked forward to this evening for a week.

But now I don't want to go. What's the matter with me, God?

I have to get through this "romantic evening." I have to discipline my mind—turn my thoughts toward politics, or literature.

It's been a long time, God, since I've been a woman first—a mother second. Tonight should be pleasurable, full of promise.

Nevertheless, my baby looks so wide-eyed and vulnerable, perched there on the sitter's arm.

Please—give them a good evening, too.

Thank you, God.

Out of Diapers

It would have been comical, God.

But it was the middle of the night. Every store in town had closed hours earlier.

The baby whimpered and tossed in his sleep, so I stumbled toward the crib to see what was wrong. He was sopping wet, virtually floating in a pale gold pool. (How do their tiny kidneys hold it all?)

I reached for a diaper—and there wasn't one.

We were out of disposables. We don't own any reusables.

His soaked, bare bottom gleamed in the moonlight; his half-awake eyes glared at me accusingly: *what are you going to do about it, Mom?*

God, this baby deserves a better mother than me. I went grocery shopping *yesterday.* I must have passed an aisle-full of disposable diapers.

Our shelves are stocked with coffee, pickles, plant fertilizer, and rice cereal tonight.

But diapers—*diapers!*—I didn't buy.

God, won't you help me to pull myself together next time?

The Visit

A childless friend came to visit me today, God.

She was immaculate. My left shoulder was caked with pablum.

She's doing graduate work. I'm doing house work.

She's read all the bestsellers. I'm lucky if I can scan a magazine in the bathtub.

I was going to have the baby clean and dressed up when she arrived—but he threw up on his new suit. When the doorbell rang, I slapped him into a fresh diaper—which he promptly soiled.

And so it went.

"Isn't he darling?" my childless friend raved.

The baby wasn't "darling" today. He was a mess. He looked unwashed and unloved.

Neither of us wanted to hold him.

My friend and her husband are having a crisis, Lord. To have a baby, or not to have a baby? I have a baby ... what do I think, *really?* Should my friend have a baby, too?

As we sipped coffee in my stacked-up kitchen, I listened as gravely as I could to her "problem," and she studied me as surreptitiously as she could, searching for a "solution."

Please help her, God, to look past the havoc in my house, into the yearnings and sensibilities of her own soul.

I don't have answers for her. As you know, I don't even have answers for myself.

A Taste of Heaven

This is the healing time of day, God.

In these quiet, shadowy hours when others sleep, I bask in the silence of this house.

If my child has had a fretful day, I watch him slumber quietly, and my love for him seems infinitely strong.

He's not a baby any longer. Stretched out beneath the blanket, his limbs seem curiously elongated.

When did he begin to grow, to mature? Why haven't I noticed these changes before now?

In these hours of the night, my perceptions are heightened. Smoothing the tousled, sandy hair of my child, peering out at your heavens from his bedroom window, I am awed by your infinity. My burgeoning problems seem insignificant.

The two of us are less than specks in your universe.

Yet, holding this little one, I feel a continuity, a rhythm, a oneness with all nature, and with you.

Thank you, God, for these quiet hours.

Thank you for silence and darkness and the warm, sleep-numbed body of this child.

Tensions are slipping away. I'm tired and happy. I feel like a part of your world. I feel that I know you as a benevolent friend, and that you care about me.

This must be a taste of heaven, God.

What's "Normal," Anyway?

This baby should be cutting teeth, God. The reference books say so. Experienced mothers say so. His doctors say so.

Yet he remains as toothless as an ancient crone. What's the matter with him?

Maybe he won't ever grow teeth.

Maybe we should have his gums X rayed.

Maybe he's not normal . . .

What *is* normal, anyway? I've grown to hate that word.

As our baby's personality unfolds, I sense he's waging a private war against normality, to see how much pandemonium he can create. He's clearly marching to a different drummer, and doesn't care whether he ever makes a deadline in his development.

You've enlightened me so many times, God. Could you help out once more, and unravel the mystery of "normal" for me?

Then give me, if you will, bright retorts for friends and acquaintances who think the time for teeth is now.

Thank you.

Special Child

They're a young couple, God. Handsome, vigorous, intelligent, sensitive.

Their new baby has a serious birth defect.

And they're shattered.

Why? Why us? They're crying out to you—and they can't hear your answer.

Numbly, they move through the first stages of shock, answering the telephone, accepting cards and flowers. Well-meaning friends don't know whether to congratulate or commiserate.

The sorrowing mother and father, so bright and graceful and witty in happier times, rely on breeding and rote etiquette to get them through the fumbling encounters.

God, please help this couple. Stand by them. Comfort them. My problems pale in comparison with theirs.

They haven't felt the full brunt of pain, yet. They haven't plumbed the depths of their grief. Eventually, they're going to have to work through difficulties they have no conception of at this time.

Show us how to lessen their pain. Tell us how we can give them even one light moment; one positive thought to cling to.

They're such special, well-beloved friends, God. They'll make a fine home for this special child of yours.

Mysterious Backache

This baby has a mysterious backache, God.
It troubles him when,
. . . a friend drops in for a visit,
. . . I'm trying to read,
. . . the house is being straightened,
. . . or he's been confined to his crib.
The backache must be terrible, judging from his whimpering and pleading.
It can be cured swiftly and completely if I pick the baby up.
That's all it takes.
Forsaking all else, and picking up the baby.
You did the exact same thing, my mother remembers, smiling, as my firstborn frets and tosses. *He'll get over it.*
So she picks him up with ineffable gentleness, and nuzzles him, and rocks him until he sleeps on her shoulder.
Thank you, God, for grandmothers.
The mysterious backache is wearing me to a frazzle.
Thank you for showing me that it will heal, in time.

Teething

It's a tense scene, God.

This teething baby is screaming in pain. His small body is rigid and taut. For the first time in recent memory, his voice has hoarsened.

He must be exhausted.

Yet he cries on and on.

And I'm about to cry, too—for there's absolutely nothing I can do to ease him.

I've tried rubbing his inflamed gums with ice and chemical preparations. I've given him rubber toys to chew on. He's had aspirin. We've rocked for miles and miles.

Wouldn't you think that medical science could ease a teething baby?

Our brisk, knowledgeable pediatric nurse sympathized briefly when I called, then said, "You're just going to have to hold out somehow. Most of our mothers need to be tranquilized far worse than the babies themselves."

So here I am, "holding out." And my nerves are about to crack.

Please, God, steady me. Lift me above this fearful din. Keep me attuned to my baby's needs, rather than concentrating on my own limitations.

Meditation for a Nose

My house was going to smell of lemon and soap and lavender sachet . . .

But the baby is spitting up. There's an ominous odor emanating from his crib.

When I finish diapering him, I'm going to have to air-blast a clogged sink. (It's full of putrifying food. The job can't wait.)

Sometimes it seems that my days are filled with loathsome tasks, God.

Why are commercial babies always rosy, powdered, and smiling? Why is my own child usually sniffling, diarrheal, and suffering from a rash?

I didn't think motherhood would smell like this. Almost every day, there's a netherland of nasty chores to plod through.

Today I feel like a charwoman—a charwoman without pay.

Yet someone has to do these things.

Some mother.

Thank you, God, for giving me the fortitude to grit my teeth, hold my nose, and get to work.

Sometimes I chuckle ruefully, remembering the imported cologne I wore at my wedding; the fragrance of the flower-filled chapel.

It's all come to this, you see—the bottom of a diaper pail.

No Sickness Allowed

Why can't mothers get sick, God?

I'm chilled and nauseous and disoriented. Aspirin isn't helping at all.

Yet as soon as I retire to bed and close my eyes, I sense a presence in the room. My husband and the baby are hunched together, forlorn, at the end of the mattress.

We were lonely for mommy . . .

For once, I'm too ill to respond and give orders. I float into a feverish sleep, and before I know what's happening, a man-sized body plops down beside me.

I feel like I'm getting a touch of something, too. Let's take a little nap.

God, if I'm sick, someone else is always sicker. Why is that?

Here I am, running this *high* temperature, and guess which of us is napping peacefully, while the baby cries?

Guess who's going to have to don a face mask and prepare a bottle? Guess who's going to have to cook dinner?

Please restore my sense of humor, God.

Help me to forgive this man for succumbing to "a touch of something," when I'm yearning to check into a hospital.

Up with Women's Rights—
How Do You Get Them, in Real Life?

I've had my consciousness raised, God. A whole new world of women's rights has opened up for me.

My husband is supportive. "Do what makes you happy," he says. Thank you for that.

But here's the problem: I'm caught and held, generationless, as I contemplate a mother's basic responsibilities.

"Get a job if you want to," my husband encouraged me. Then he disappeared on a business trip. Once more, I was left behind with you and the baby.

When a job materialized, I had my choice between baby-sitters, day care centers, and housekeepers; I tried each of them in turn.

Then the baby became sick, and no one would take care of him—no one except me.

"It's policy," the day care center's manager explained.

"I might catch something," the housekeeper said.

"At my age, it's dangerous, dear," the elderly sitter told me.

"My mother won't let me," the younger sitter lamented.

When I apologized to my brand-new boss, the best he could manage was an irritated, "If you must."

Equal rights make such good sense to me, Lord.

How do mothers get them, in real life?

Playpen

Yesterday it seemed big enough. The baby had plenty of room to stretch out and crawl a few paces in any direction.

Today the playpen seems to have shrunk. Whenever I try to lower the baby into it, his face turns beet-red and he howls with rage.

He's ready, you see, for the floor—and all its attendant dangers. He wants to search for dustballs, probe light sockets, and bang his knees against the hardwood.

What do I do now, God? How can I best ease him into this new freedom?

The playpen looks more protective and snug than ever before.

I really hate to put it away.

But it's an obsolete haven, isn't it, God?

Whimsical One

Hyperactive. Temperamental. Irritable.
No one seems to have a good word for the one-year-old, God.

Just the same, I relish the age.

With all their foibles, year-old babies have the redeeming grace of humor.

Their faces mug outrageously.

They cackle with glee when you tickle them.

Their mischief is outsized, calculated to enrage. They are *so* terrible that you have to laugh—or cry.

I chose to laugh long ago. One-year-olds are funny people, all right, and laughter is the only way to coexist with them, and keep your sanity.

Laughter is the great leveller.

If you laugh at a year-old baby, he'll stop what he's doing, and laugh back.

Thank you, God, for making these babies comical.

Otherwise, there wouldn't be much to recommend them.

The Responsibility Prayer

A family is hurting, God.

Their grown-up daughter dropped out of school, drifted from job to job, experimented with drugs, and floundered through a string of empty relationships.

At twenty, she looks and acts like a street-wise thirty-year-old. And I, who knew her as a child, am saddened by her pathetic new hardness.

Her parents blame "the times" for what happened to their daughter. They've told me to expect the same behavior from my own children someday.

The times have changed, they repeat until they are lulled out of guilt. *The times . . . it's the times.*

And because we were in their home as guests, I sat silently, and let them say what they would.

But a great rage welled up inside me.

I deny their premise that my children are doomed to failure by an unsettled society.

I refuse to believe that parents can't battle "the times."

Help me, Lord.

The Survival Prayer

Why did you give me an active, inquiring mind, God?

Why did you allow my love for study to grow?

Why did you show me new worlds in books? Endow me with travel-lust? Make me hunger for education?

I'm just a mother now, Lord.

Money is tight. The baby is fretful. My body has lost its slender girlishness. I feel second-rate.

All around me, people are achieving.

My husband's career is soaring.

And I—I have no career at all.

I'm only a mother now . . .

My career is spooning strained cereal into a baby's mouth. Television is my closest companion. I'm too tired to read at night. I'm boring, even to myself.

This is a survival prayer, God.

For the first time in my life, I hate to wake up in the morning.

Help me. Please help me to rediscover the joy of living. Help me to be creative. Help me to overcome fatigue and despair.

I used to be a worthwhile person; I want to be worthwhile again.

This is the path I chose, God; this is the life I coveted.

Please show me how to concentrate once more on the dynamic, fulfilling, exciting aspects of motherhood. I'm floundering, and I can't seem to find my way back to you alone.

Please, God, help me to find my way.

Please love me.

Please fill me with resolve.

Please help me to be strong and brave.

This is a survival prayer, Lord.

Let me find a sense of purpose in sustaining the life of my child.

And let me rediscover that essential part of myself that makes me unique . . . not somebody's wife, somebody's mother, somebody's daughter.

Daily, I ask your blessings on my family; on other people in need of your help.

Today, though, I'm making a personal petition, from the depths of my soul.

This is a survival prayer, Lord—a private prayer, to you from me.

Pregnant Again

I'm pregnant again, God; I'm trying hard to be civil about it.

This is, after all, a planned child.

Nevertheless, now that the plan is consummated, I find myself panicking: *what could we have been thinking of?*

I'd forgotten so many things. The morning nausea . . . the craving for long naps . . . the aching and muscle cramps . . . the anxiety that something might be wrong with the baby . . .

What a destructive frame of mind, God! I should be affirming the rightness, the joyousness of this decision.

I should be looking forward to the new family member, instead of brooding about my own pain.

I should be hiding my reservations, instead of dwelling on them morbidly.

Won't you shake me out of this self-indulgent depression, God?

Two

How many children are we going to have?

There are decisions—and then there are cross-roads, God.

My husband and I passed a crossroad today.

Not long ago, we couldn't have had this talk. Our family would have expanded until my body was taxed to excess. People bred continually, because that's what custom dictated.

Then came the advent of birth control—and some of the hardest decision making you've entrusted us with to date.

We explored every facet of family planning today. We weighed the limits of the earth's bounty, and the limits of our household budget. We spoke of emotional and spiritual considerations, and frankly determined our breaking points.

Then, God, we came to our decision.

Two babies is enough—for us. Some gifted parents should have more than two . . . perhaps an unlimited number of children. Some people should never become parents at all.

But given our own particular natures, our resources, and our hopes for the future—two is the right number.

Thank you for moving technology forward, so that all children can be wanted ones.

As I sit here, ripe with pregnancy, stroking the silky hair of my firstborn child, I feel a glow of optimism for the years ahead. I sense the rightness of our decision. I sense —at least I hope—that our plan pleases you.

Second Chance

I can't believe it, Lord!

I just had a baby--and I feel wonderful!

As difficult as the first delivery was—that's how easy and comfortable this one seemed.

I knew what to expect this time. I wasn't paralyzed by fear.

The pains, when they came, seemed rhythmic and natural and perfectly in harmony with your plan.

I was thinking about the baby this time, instead of my own discomfort, my own fears, and the host of small indignities that are heaped on delivering mothers.

Thank you, God, for letting me experience a beautiful, simple birth.

Thank you for the perfect baby that resulted.

Thank you for the radiant face of my husband—he couldn't be with me when our firstborn arrived. Thank you for the firm, comforting grip of his hand as the baby came to meet us.

What a glorious experience! I'm absolutely elated. I've never felt better.

I sense that you are sharing in my joy; warming me with your wonderful, healing presence.

Oh, God. What a rare day. What an unspeakably beautiful day . . .

Have I told you lately that I love you?

One Baby, Two Babies

"What was the difference between one baby and two babies?" a friend asked me. "You already had a child —so your life-style didn't change much, right?"

Wrong. Oh, God—that is *so* wrong!

I never realized how manageable one baby is, until there were two.

I never realized how inexpensive one child is, until we had a second.

Where before, I could reserve an hour to read, or listen to good music, or restore an antique—now I have bare minutes to pursue adult interests.

Before this second child was born, I had visions of myself efficiently synchronizing naps, lunches, and diaper changes.

What a fool I was, God!

Each of them has an individual time clock, and they're stubbornly set on opposing schedules.

When one is hungry, the other dawdles. When one is asleep, the other lies wide awake. When one is playful, the other is languid and cuddly.

Sometimes I look at them, and marvel that they could come from the same genetic line. How different they are, in every way! Their dispositions are wildly diverse— one is pensive, the other a clown.

We had the second baby because we wanted a companion for our first. But I don't think these two even like each other very much. They quarrel and compete until I don't feel like a mother at all. I more closely resemble a diplomat, endlessly negotiating settlements.

Help me to steer these two young lives into some semblance of accord, God.

For a Grown-Up Friend

God bless you . . .
>. . . for humoring my child,
>. . . for listening to him,
>. . . for making him feel important.

God keep you . . .
>. . . for remembering his likes and dislikes,
>. . . for knowing the name of his nursery
> teacher,
>. . . for buying a box of raisins just for him,
> and keeping them in a place only you and
> he know.

God cherish you . . .
>. . . for hugging him when you meet,
>. . . for smoothing his stubborn hair,
>. . . for gently brushing his tear-stained lashes.

God cheer you . . .
>. . . for smiling at his ridiculous bouts of
> bravado,
>. . . for expecting him to be "somebody,"
>. . . for treating him like a human being,
> instead of an appendage to me.

God ease you . . .
>. . . for never talking down to him,
>. . . for keeping his secrets,
>. . . for realizing that beneath the scruffy exterior
> of this child,
> beats the heart of a true friend,
> and as much love as you could wish for
> in a lifetime of yearning.

The Weak of the Earth

I'm not sick today, God. But I'm so tired. So run-down. So utterly drained of vitality.

Without my constant attention, how could these children manage? I feed them, bathe them, dress them, entertain them.

If they fill a diaper or crawl out of sight, I have to drop everything I'm doing and attend to them.

Oh God, I'm so tired of it all. The aching weariness. The sameness of my days. Their incessant demands on my time.

Sometimes I fantasize about running away from home, and starting all over again. I dream about careers, attractive clothes, trips to interesting places, meals in quiet restaurants.

Other women have broken away. I suppose I could, too.

But guilt, and a sense of duty, and real love for my husband and children anchor me to this routine . . .

Bless me with energy, God. Make me equal to my many responsibilities. Renew my conviction that life is worth struggling through, and that time will ease the struggle.

I'm really hurting. Really disaffected and wrung out. Won't you help me, please?

This Test Will Tell Us
Something Someday

I'm a guinea pig in a psychological experiment, God.

A kindly Ph.D. is seated across from me, asking me questions in a soft, professional monotone.

Do I get headaches? Do I get along well with my husband? Do I ever hear strange noises?

Yes. Yes. No.

We're having an interesting time, Lord. I'm sort of enjoying the test, wondering what the questions are *really* asking, and wondering whether my answers are the "right" ones.

Then the psychologist goes for blood.

Do you have children? *Yes.*

How many? *Two.*

What sex? *Boy and girl.*

If you could be doing anything in the world you wanted to be doing, what would it be? Would you be a mother? *Silence, I'm thinking . . .*

Would you be a mother? *Silence.* (I'm recalling my university days; wandering, unencumbered, around the beautiful campus. I'm thinking of studying late and impromptu coffee parties and no babyfilled backpack on my aching back.)

Would you have children? *Silence.*

Would you have children? Go on—say it! You can tell me!

"No," I whisper, horror-struck before the word is articulated. "No . . . not today, I wouldn't. But I *would* . . . other times. You see, I *love* my children. I'd *die* for my children, if I had to . . . ."

"I didn't ask whether you love them," the psychologist says, seeming to take a perverse delight in my discomfort. "I didn't ask whether you'd die for them."

I look at the floor, appalled.

"There, was that so hard?" the psychologist asks, beguiling. "Many women feel that way. Many, many women feel that way . . ."

I look at him, begging with my eyes. For what?

Oh, God, I love my children. I do. I thank you for them daily. And yet . . .

Fleetingly, I think of my very nice pre-married life. I yearn to go back to it, sometimes, when the going gets rough. I'd like, once in a while, to timetravel backwards.

Do my memories, my secret yearnings, make me an inferior mother, God? I haven't eradicated the girl who was, or the woman who might have been. They dance before me maddeningly sometimes, taunting me, mocking the housewife I've become.

Yet I love my home. I love my children. I love marriage.

Conflict, God, is the stuff of my life these days.

"I sense an undercurrent of anger in you," the psychologist says—and smiles.

Why shouldn't I be angry, God? This man has induced me to wrestle with the ultimate question, the question prudent mothers don't ever ask themselves.

I had these babies. They're here. I love them now.

Isn't that enough for him, God?

Isn't that enough for you?

Licking the Floor

God, my baby's licking the floor.

I just can't believe it.

There he lies on his stomach (where I put him for just a moment), flailing his arms and legs and contentedly lapping the linoleum.

When you were passing out the talents, why was I made a bookworm, instead of a compulsive floor-polisher? My flesh crawls, thinking of the germs breeding within reach of the baby's tongue.

The irony is that I love an immaculate home. It would be so soothing, so uplifting, to end each day in a glistening, freshly-waxed room, free of dust . . . free of the children's clutter.

Each time I begin to scrub anew, however, I'm diverted from the task at hand. A child cries. An argument erupts. An accident happens.

So the floors are polished erratically.

My home, and my life, continue on a casual course.

Oh, God. I've heard that everyone eats a peck of dirt in his lifetime, but when I see something like this, I feel so remorseful. So literally unclean.

Please replace some of this flagging energy. Let me organize myself and my home a little better in the future.

Terrible Two

The twos are just as terrible as we'd been warned, God.

The negativism, the hyperactivity, the temper tantrums—they're all making an appearance.

For some reason, I thought if I worked hard enough at mothering, the transition from one to three would be smooth and effortless.

It just didn't happen that way.

My baby's standing here now, lip thrust out, arms crossed, prime for a spanking.

I want to reestablish the closeness we had a few months ago, when he found all the security he needed in the circle of my arms.

But it's not to be. That time has passed.

His days are a jumble of raucous *no's,* pointless rebellion, and destruction.

My love for him is tinged with resentment and exasperation.

Keep us from growing too far apart, God. It's going to be a difficult year.

Bring Out the Musical Potty
and We Can Dance

I used to love baroque music, God. Chamber music.

Nowadays, my favorite strains come from the chamber pot.

These musical potties are a miracle of technology. If my baby remembers where to position himself before filling the pot, we all get to hear "London Bridge."

It's not your symphony-in-the-park, exactly, but it's the next best thing . . .

"London Bridge" is the freedom song for me.

"London Bridge" means shopping in a department store, unafraid.

"London Bridge" means nursery-school admission and Sunday-school promotion. Training pants instead of diapers. A more civilized home. Better smells in the crib.

I expected that toilet training would be difficult, but it hasn't been. We just brought out the musical potty . . . and danced with glee every time it played.

Thank you, God, for "London Bridge."

Thank you for this fine-looking, intelligent baby; this highly-motivated musician.

Someday, he may be conducting an orchestra somewhere; who knows? Years from now, we might be sitting front row center, watching a grown-up baby direct an overture.

I doubt, however, that his future musical feats can compete with the first thrilling, on-target "London Bridge." *Welcome to civilization,* we exulted when the song began.

Thank you, God.

That's Mine

That's mine!

I don't ever want to hear those words again, God.

Our home resounds with that phrase. Once the children utter it, an argument always follows.

That's mine! Spite and anger and cruelty surface, as soon as they begin to squabble over possessions.

Why do they behave this way? We're not affluent, but there is enough of almost everything to go around. Sharing is anathema to them.

They simply refuse to pool their belongings. They prefer to divide, and hide, and declare boundaries and limits . . . .

Don't go in there—that's my room!

Oh, God, I'm so tired of this.

I'm so sick of their nitpicking and fighting.

We've tried to rear them properly. We've given them time, not just material things.

Nevertheless, something went wrong, somewhere along the line.

Help me to solve this problem, before it destroys their relationship.

Show me how to assume a mother's role once more.

I'm so weary of acting as their referee.

End of the Perfect Nursery Hunt

They don't have to hug my son and daughter.

They don't have to compliment them.

They don't have to laugh with them or tease them.

But love doesn't cost extra here, in this house of children.

Everyone gets love—the shy child, the hyperactive child, the minority child, the newcomer.

Everyone gets love.

Even when the noise seems intolerable and the children are tired and fretful . . . I feel the love in this nursery.

Even when the teachers are worried about problems of their own . . . the healing force of love strengthens them and blesses their efforts here.

Thank you for leading us to this school, and these teachers.

Thank you for the care my children receive, and the tenderness with which it is administered.

Cruelty

Why is it, God, that I can face almost any disappointment for myself—but when the children are hurt, I go to pieces?

They are hurt so often!

They are teased maliciously, excluded from play, and called names. Then they run home, telling me all about it as they wipe their tear-splattered faces.

I feel such pain when they are unhappy, God.

I have such grief when I am powerless to help them in their children's world.

There is a darker side of the problem, too. For when they are "on top" and popular, inevitably another playmate is home and crying.

I love my children—but I don't idealize them.

I realize only too well that they, too, torment and tease their neighbors. I've heard them do it, just as I've heard it done to them.

Sometimes it seems like an endless chain of battles and reconciliations.

Why are children so cruel to each other?

Why are *people* so cruel to each other?

Can't we ever change, God?

Wait Till the Children Are Grown; There's Plenty of Time . . .

There was a first, faint tang of autumn in the air, God. Three of us had slipped outdoors to watch the brown-bordered leaves as they fell. As women will, we congregated in a central yard, broke out the coffee mugs, and enjoyed an impromptu visit.

"How are you doing?" a kindly friend asked.

It was the moment to nod; to murmur a perfunctory "fine." But her lively blue eyes blazed with interest and animation; I sensed she really wanted to know.

Before I could contain myself, a torrent of emotion was unleashed. *Sick babies! Bills! Fatigue!*

And with infinite care and empathy they listened, my two beloved neighbors. They nodded and clucked and chuckled until my tide of words was stemmed with a frantic: *What should I do?*

An unsettling silence followed, God. They quit smiling; they didn't know what to say.

Then my next-door neighbor cleared her throat; a young mother herself, she was painfully familiar with the restlessness, the discontent I had voiced. "Break out," she urged. "You were a smart girl [*were!*]. Do something with yourself. Get a job, anything. The years go by, and it doesn't get easier."

What a disquieting thought! I never realized it before, but I had counted heavily on the years going by . . . and "things," those nebulous, nameless irritations, falling right into place.

They're not going to, are they, God? My life will go on . . . and when the problems of my children's extreme youth are resolved, other problems—problems of a different nature—will be waiting to ensnare me.

It was a disturbing insight, but I thank you for it. I'd been marking off these days and weeks, not even trying to live them to the fullest. I'd been waiting for solutions to drop, unbidden, into my lap. I haven't even tried to re-arrange or improve my life . . . "time" was going to take care of that.

Thank you for telling me, in this way, that we each have our measure of days, and that even the most turbu-lent and troubled of them are to be valued.

Together, Alone

It's silent, and dark outside. The babies are sleeping. And I'm so lonely.

My husband, who goes on business trips, has embarked on yet another one. So I'm solitary tonight, roaming through the still house, wanting someone, *anyone,* to call me up—to remember that I'm alive.

The telephone's not ringing, God.

Nobody's remembering.

I go to the bookshelves, and thumb through volume after volume, searching for something to capture my interest, as long as nobody's going to keep me company.

But I've already read these books, God—most of them twice. The only book here I haven't read is a lengthy, mind-improving one. I'm not equal to it tonight—I'm not up to much of anything.

I could go telephone a friend or relative, but the idea of initiating a conversation turns me off. I don't feel like being the *caller*—I want to be the *called.* If I contacted anyone tonight, what excuse could I offer for interrupting them? The women I know are probably enjoying the companionship of their husbands, after the day's separation. A lone woman with two infants doesn't fit into anyone's evening plans.

How can you come right out and blurt, "I need somebody tonight"? That's just a little naked for my tastes, God. I'm a private person. It's agony for me to expose my own loneliness to another of your children. I have some good friends, but I don't have *many* friends. I don't even *want* many friends.

Still . . . tonight, I wish I were more of a "people person." I wish I had a houseful of laughing, loving, caring souls, to warm the chill isolation of this house.

The babies are down for the night, but I may slip

into bed with my oldest one, for just a minute, to hear his even breathing; to nuzzle his moist, tousled curls.

Where are you tonight, God?

As a parent, encumbered with the custody of two small children, I haven't the freedom to go out, searching for diversion; looking for another life to touch.

Won't you come in, God? Won't you sit with me awhile?

I think I'll brew a cup of tea and read that fat, pretentious book.

While I'm puttering around, looking for a cup and saucer, would you still this aching, restless feeling, Lord?

I've got everything I need within these walls, yet I still feel incomplete. Won't you give me some signal that I'm not all alone with these sleeping infants?

Am I Really Over the Hill, God?

I'm visiting with a young relative, God.

We're talking, and the babies are bucking and fussing on the carpet, a wild, moving tangle of arms and legs.

It should be a happy, domestic scene—but it's not.

Though only a few years separate us, this young girl is worlds apart from me, in life-style, in dress, in language, in priorities.

She thinks I'm over the hill, God—the message is coming through loud and clear, past her empty smile and bored eyes.

This is a duty call for her. Someone made her come. The babies and I are her good deed for the day.

I should be grateful for the company, and the respite from household drudgery, but I'm not—I'm furious. I want to shake my guest and shout, "Youth doesn't last forever! Be arrogant about anything but your youth, because time flies . . . "

Someday, I hope we can be good friends. That would make me happy. It would please our families, too.

But now, God—now it's futile to pretend that we enjoy each other's company.

When we visit these days, I patiently listen to her hopes and dreams for the future—it's understood that I have no dreams, no future. My future is *now*—and it's dreary. Motherhood is dreary. Married life is dreary. My whole mode of living frightens her . . . she wants something "different"; something "better," she says.

Help her, God. Help her to feel at ease in her role as a woman. Help her to explore her options, without condemning those who have chosen other life-styles, other paths.

You know, God, that I don't envy her youth. Adolescence was a dreadful time for me—I couldn't wait to outgrow it.

I suppose, though, I *am* jealous of her zest for life, her unclouded vision of the future, her bubbling self-confidence.

She's been sheltered, God. She hasn't known much pain or anxiety or fear. Her parents—also "over the hill" —have buffered life for her, until she sees it in glorious, uncompromised terms of black-and-white . . . no gray; not yet, anyway.

I wish that during these interminable visits, we could *say* something to each other. I wish I could show her the happy, positive side of maturing—for there is one. I wish I could help her to conquer youth-worship—that fixation is bound to end in heartbreak. I wish I could reach out and touch the person she really is—or better yet, the woman she might be someday.

Will you help her to see I'm not her enemy, God?

As she gets ready to assume her place in the adult world, will you bless her with adult perspectives?

She's family, God—and that means a lot to me. Right now, though, we can't communicate.

Patience Aplenty Wanted Here

My nerves are shot, God.

I'm holding on to a thin, fragile thread of calm. For days now, my prayers have been incoherent outbursts: "Help me! Please, please help me!"

The household routine is so dull, so grinding, so confining. It's finally whipped me. I can't mobilize sufficiently to call a baby-sitter, to escape even for a short time.

Every day seems just like the day before. The same chores reappear over and over again. So what's the point of all this?

Can you tell me?

Even the creative aspect of staying at home—my time with the children—has degenerated into a maintenance problem. My arms are never still. They diaper, feed, bathe, dress, undress, clean up, soothe . . .

Look at me. Look at what I've become. The travel, the university work are no longer apparent. No one would want to meet me, to talk with me. I look dispirited, run-down, ashen, gaunt.

I look like thousands of other young mothers . . .

Please. Shake me out of this depression. Show me something . . . anything . . . meaningful about housework.

Tension, Tension

I thought I was dying ahead of schedule, Lord.

Sharp, excruciating pains shot through my abdomen. My head hurt so badly I wanted to scream.

Alarmed, I rushed to a doctor.

"You're not dying, don't worry," he said. "It's tension. That's all."

He offered me a choice between pain and tranquilizers.

I took the tranquilizers.

So many of my friends have "tension," God.

We sit in our kitchens like so many Librium queens, regally detached from the chaos that surrounds us, eyes glazed, bodies limp and relaxed . . . out of pain, at last.

I don't want to be drug-dependent, God. I want to be tranquil . . . not tranquilized.

I want to see things clearly, in needle-sharp focus, not through an artificial, chemical film.

Won't you help me to conquer tension, Lord? Perhaps I'm being too idealistic, but I can't believe you and I can't beat this thing, somehow.

Please help me to relax, to unwind, to neutralize the small crises that are making me ill.

Thank you, Lord.

My Job, Your Job

Both of us had had wretched days, God. Our faces were mirror-images of fatigue, frustration, and despair.

When we fell into bed, tense, aching, and yearning for sleep . . . the baby began to cry.

"I'll get him," my husband murmured, in a tone that really said, *I'm so tired, I can't move, you do it* . . .

"Don't bother," I snapped, resentful of his work day outside the confining walls of this house.

No one in the world could have kept me from playing the martyr that night.

Martyred—that's really the way I see myself these days.

We're playing a destructive game, God: "My Job, Your Job." No longer do we think in terms of *ours*—life is compartmentalized. My responsibility. Your responsibility. My baby. Your career. My home. Your outside world.

I hate this—but I don't know how to stop.

God, listen! Show us how to pull together again. I need help from this man so badly, yet I've forgotten how to ask for it. When he offers to tend the baby, or to clean the house, I've forgotten how to accept graciously. I retreat into a shell of pride: *my job, mine!*

Teach us how to share work, and the rewards of work. Enable us, please, to labor side by side for the good of our family.

Where Do We Go After Here?

We visited my grandfather today, God.

In a quarter-century, his comfortable creek-side home has not changed much. It has mellowed, evolved, become more at one with the land—aging much as a person might.

Memories engulfed me as I watched my children scurry through wooded paths I had explored two decades earlier. For a moment, I was depressed by the feeling that we are only a flash in time.

Then my pensive mood fell away; four generations of our family hiked back to Grandfather's warm, memory-filled house.

As we walked, my daughter asked the question I had dreaded to hear: "Where's Meema? I haven't seen her; where's my Meema?"

My throat constricted; just days ago Grandfather's wife of fifty years passed away, quietly, with a minimum of fuss—the way she always wanted it.

"Where's Meema?" she asked again. "Where's Meema today?"

And I wanted to shout: *You* tell her! *You* explain it to her! *You* make her understand, Lord!

I fumbled for the words, and ended up passing on Sunday-school homilies that seemed to suffice. It was difficult, though, to speak of heaven and the reward of death, when our family circle is so painfully incomplete.

How would you explain death to a little child? How can I? How long must we wait before this awful hurt eases?

Talk to me, God.

Children and Warmth

It's Saturday morning, God.

The children have stumbled out of their own beds and crept into ours. For a few moments, we shiver together as rain and sleet gently pelt the roof of the house.

Then our little girl begins her Song of the Early Morning. In a sweet, meandering soprano, she improvises:

If Mom would get up I could have breakfast,
I could have sugar bear cereal or maybe eggs,
Or maybe Daddy would get doughnuts before we
starve,
La-la, Brother and I are real hungry, la-laaaaa.

I don't remember when her morning songs first began. The lyrics change from week to week, but they're always inspired by the emptiness of her stomach (and her brother's; she looks after his interests too).

You'd better make some coffee for your
sleepies . . .

She keeps caroling new verses until her father and I are nudged into wakefulness.

It's a warm, happy way to begin the morning, God. Having seen these children through midnight feedings and an infinity of diaper changes, we're beginning to reap some of the rewards of parenthood. How I relish these intimate moments with my family!

Thank You for this boy and girl. They are love and light and the still-fresh core of our older, more jaded souls.

Love Thy Neighbor

In play, they are always fighting, God.

They "kill" each other with toy guns, and if their guns are taken away, they improvise with sticks.

Either way, the killing goes on.

Some child always ends up "dead."

I'm not particularly enchanted with war games. My husband spent a year at war. A quarter-century earlier, my father was battling in a foreign country.

When I look at my young son, a cold fear grips me, God.

When will his turn come? Must it come?

Sometimes I want to round up all the toy guns in this neighborhood, and bury them deep beneath the earth. A friend of mine disagrees, and raises some valid points.

Won't my children need to learn self-defense? Won't a school bully find them an easy mark, otherwise? Won't they be destroyed, if they have to face the real world from a cocoon of idealism?

Who's right, God?

I really don't know. Mulling the problem over, I can justify either point of view. My friend is right. I'm right. We're both right.

Children need toughness to grow, to survive. Just the same, I can't help wondering if we're not planting the seeds for later wars, by encouraging them to battle each other from infancy. On television, they always see war portrayed as high adventure.

It's not adventure, God. It's as close to hell as mortals get. And we do it to ourselves.

Am I making a mountain out of a molehill?

This one is too tough for me. I'm too emotionally involved to see straight.

Show me the answer.

The Bath

This used to be the sanctum sanctorum, God: the bathroom.

I seem to remember a time when I could luxuriate in a hot, scented bath—alone.

It's a whole different ball game now.

Cannily, I select moments when the babies are immersed in play, or taking naps, or visiting with their father. Then I sneak into the bathroom, turn the knobs, let hot water rush into the tub—and there they are. Two round, curious faces, peering over the porcelain tub, watching my every move.

They want to visit, God—or so they tell me.

If I evict them, they scream. If I spank them for screaming, they howl louder, and any pleasure I could have derived from the steaming water, the solitude, and the methodical cleansing goes . . . forgive me, Lord . . . down the drain.

What's so fascinating about a mother in the bathroom, Lord? These babies don't plague their father when he's shaving, or using the toilet, or singing in the shower. They don't offer him soap, or toilet paper, or bath toys. Just me.

God, please let me take a bath. Alone. Uninterrupted.

Let me squander a little bath oil on myself; let me sneak a paperback book past these two vigilantes, reading, perhaps, a couple of pages in the tub.

A bath alone would be so soothing, Lord. So rejuvenating.

I'm turning the water on now. Could you let it run very, very quietly today?

Demolition Derby

These babies are trying to destroy our home and everything in it, God—including themselves.

I feel that we are all participating in a demolition derby.

Proud of their new mobility, these crawling, toddling commandos crash through carefully erected barriers, bent on demolishing the furniture, the objets d'art, and my peace of mind.

They'd plug each other into the electrical outlets, if they could. They'd play football with the Wedgwood.

Forgive me for the times, when—childless—I berated couples for "babyproofing" their homes.

The old quotes are tormenting me now: "When I have children, I'm not stripping *my* house down to plastic covers and bare tabletops . . . "

I was a fool, God, and worse—an opinionated fool.

As I sit, tensed for the next emergency, sensing waiting dangers in my house of the plastic covers, I beg you for help.

Motherhood is the land of unrest. Just when I think I've spotted all the perils, still another looms, in the guise of something sharp, or hot, or serrated, ready to rend young flesh.

Strengthen me in this vigil, God.

Open my eyes, quicken my senses, keep me one step ahead of these vigorous, inventive babies of mine.

Prayer for the Open Road

What an unholy din, God!

What a cacophony of shrill, whining infant voices!

I'm trying to negotiate a very dangerous freeway. Trucks and cars spurt past me, honking impatiently, as I hug the right-hand side of the road—the "slow" side.

The babies seem to be engaged in a conspiracy to break my concentration; to get us all killed.

"Quiet!!!" I shout.

The anger in my voice spurs them on to new, unexplored peaks of hysteria.

I'm ready to drag out all the ugly oaths I've ever heard. So I utter one, taking grim satisfaction in this small sin, this maverick word—and my son pounces on it, repeats it gleefully, rolling his tongue over the earthy syllable. (Making it, I know, a permanent part of his limited vocabulary—a mirror of our family discussions at home.)

Oh, my God! Please get us home in one piece.

Please, please make these babies hush up. Let their little mouths lock tightly together, just once. Let silence prevail.

I love them both. You know I do. Still, right now my hand is tingling to wallop them. I want to pull the car over and spank the nearest child. (It doesn't matter which one, I'll get them both eventually.) Yet there's no way to stop.

I have to keep driving, keep moving. I have to stay within "the flow of traffic."

I know you're *supposed* to be everywhere, God. Are you in the flow of traffic, too?

Grammy and Grand-Dad

The babies are packed for a visit to their grandparents, God. They're cleaner than usual, scoured and slicked down and buttoned into fresh clothing.

I suspect that the children's invitation was prompted by a visit I had with my parents yesterday. They didn't say much, but they took everything in: my wild expression, unkempt hair, and the strained spinach spots on my blouse.

Usually, Grammy and Grand-Dad concentrate on the babies, picking them up and cuddling them and teaching them new words. Yesterday, though, they sensed that I was desperate for some adult conversation. So we visited as we used to, and the children napped. By the time they left, I felt refreshed, reawakened to the world, momentarily lifted above the pressures and the uproar of this lively house.

I could have wept with relief, when my mother said, glancing at my father, "Could we have them tomorrow, for a day or two? Yes, I'm sure. Oh, it would do us good . . ."

I don't know if the visit will really do them good, Lord—but it will be a breath of fresh air for me. Soon— tomorrow!—I'll have a respite, a chance to regroup, an opportunity to immerse myself in silence and adult pursuits. It will renew my appreciation of the babies. I'll miss them. I'll be aching to hold them, by the time they come tumbling and shouting back to our home.

Thank you for grandparents, thank you for their sensitivity, their encouragement, their help, but most of all, for their selflessness. They remember, God. I can tell.

God's Good Groceries

I feel like an old tugboat, with barnacles clinging to my unpainted hull.

Only I'm navigating the aisle of a grocery store, God—and the barnacles are my children.

While other shoppers steer their neatly stacked carts past us, my toddlers are tackling my legs and dragging on their bellies behind me.

"Shame!" an elegant, white-haired lady hisses, as she presents her one lamb chop to the checker.

Everyone in the store is watching us; waiting, I suspect, to see if I'll haul off and hit my companions.

I probably should.

Oh, God! Why couldn't I afford a sitter today? Why can't you check children like packages, at a store's entrance?

I'm burning with embarrassment. Furthermore, I'm confused.

My children are usually well-behaved. They rarely step out of line in public.

Why did they lose control today?

Great Day

Somehow, today, we mustered the energy to get up early.

Before we knew it, my husband and I were working side by side, cleaning the house. In an hour it was gleaming and orderly.

We felt restless and wanted to do something fun with the babies. So we slipped on our backpacks—with the babies in them—and struck out for the park.

The fresh air felt great, God. There was a nip in the air, and we enjoyed the coolness, the sunshine, and the feeling of taxing our lethargic muscles.

By expending a little effort, we had a great day; a healthy day. We turned off the mindless, flickering television set, and it stayed off.

We talked and played together.

We walked through scattered banks of leaves, listening to the brittle crunch beneath our shoes.

Each of us marvelled, in his own way, at the beauty of the new season.

What a wonderful time we had, God!

And it didn't cost a cent . . . that's the amazing thing.

To Spank or Not to Spank?

The children need to be punished sometimes, God. Years ago, we vowed to stand united when we were correcting them.

Unfortunately, the vow hasn't withstood the test of time.

My husband thinks I'm not strict enough.

I think he's *too* strict.

So we're in the middle of a standoff.

As a result, I've become "the savior" in the family —the soft touch. And their father is "the grouch."

The children are becoming ever more skilled at pitting us against each other, to gain their own ends. It's an impossible situation.

God, I know this is destructive. My husband is disgusted at our vacillations, and I'm getting that way.

Please, in the future, help us to reach accord on when to spank, how to spank . . . or whether to spank at all.

Thank you.

Free Speech and Other Evils

Dear God, now that my children are talking so clearly and so well, please let them use discretion in their speech.

Help them keep what diminutive family skeletons we have in the closet, where they belong.

Give them the strength to refrain from loud editorial comment when adults are assembled—for adult conversation.

Steer them, oh God, into the still waters of silence, as regards their mother's housekeeping tribulations, the latest neighborhood feud, or the facts of life.

Show them that quiet contemplation has sweet rewards. Gently guide them past the pitfalls of preschool namecalling; keep them from vivid descriptions of the "last time Daddy got mad at Mommy," when they confide in their beloved nursery teacher.

I never put much stock in censorship, and when the children are older—when they have developed judgment —I pray they can enjoy free speech.

Just now, though, God . . . just now, could you help me to explain to them the difference between matters public and private?

Naptime

My children are bundled into their beds this afternoon, limp as a pair of rag dolls. They had a vigorous morning of play, and though they protested mightily at the idea of a nap, I lured them between the sheets so they could "rest and look at books." Ten minutes later, they were snoring, oblivious to the cloth volumes dangling from their small, insensate fists.

Thank you, God, for naptime. I'd like to take a nap, too, but these moments are too precious to waste in sleep. Softly, in my bare feet, I glide around the house, accomplishing tasks these two nappers would want to help me with if they were awake.

It's a drowsy, pleasant time of day. Even though I'm throbbing with weariness, I'm determined to stay alert for the rare, elusive peacefulness that descends upon this house when the children are in residence—but suspended in sleep.

Naptime is really the best of both worlds, God. I feel as free as a childless woman, but the children are here, unspeakably appealing as they rest. As they lie curled beneath their blankets, I feel as if I'm on a small vacation. My soul is weary and I crave quiet. Quiet, above all things . . .

Thank you, God, for lifting me above the cheerful bedlam these children manufacture during the day. Thank you for sealing their eyes and hushing them, for just a short time.

Thank you, too, for waking them up again. Here they come, the prototypes of grouchiness, rubbing their eyes, and crossly whining for me. It's time to pick up two little children and two wet, ragged Teddy bears, and head for the nearest rocking chair.

Go Away

I was stunned, God.

We were entertaining someone we hadn't seen in a long time.

He had never met our children. And how we looked forward to introducing them!

Yet when the moment arrived, our expectations were shattered. Our friend, it seems, isn't fond of the young. Our son and daughter were an interruption, and he let them know it.

Their faces fell, and they made a quick retreat . . . no doubt wondering what they had done wrong.

God, this is a prayer for kindness.

Let us welcome children into our hearts; let us make a place for them, and comfort them when they feel anxious or inadequate.

Let us be sensitive to their needs, and soothe them as they begin the long transition from the nursery to adulthood.

I know, God, that every visit shouldn't be transformed into a children's hour. I realize that adults crave adult company, and sometimes a child is an intrusion.

When we do invite them to join us, however . . . please let compassionate friends ease their way.

Thank you.

Getting Ready for Church

Between you and me, Lord, I'm going to try to pull off the impossible tomorrow morning. I'm going to try to get these children ready for church—on time.

I don't know why, but it seems as if we're constantly late, slinking into the very last pew, long after the ushers have discreetly shut the doors.

It wasn't always like this, Lord. Before the children were born—before diaper bags, and spit-up cereal, and mismatched socks—my husband and I used to arrive in the sanctuary early. Those were wonderful moments for quiet meditation, for prayer, for thinking through the problems of the week.

Now, however, no matter how hard I try to organize in advance, my timetable falls apart on Sunday morning.

Breakfast milk sours.

Shoes get lost, or outgrown overnight.

The telephone rings.

The cat runs away.

God, please help me to get the four of us to church this week—dressed and fed and receptive to your word.

I know I can do it. I *know* I can.

My intentions are good . . . my adrenalin is racing . . . we have fourteen hours until church tomorrow.

Did I leave enough time?

Reminders

Help me, God. I've turned into a chronic nag.

Wash your hands. Flush the toilet. Pick up your toys.

I've been scattering orders automatically, without stopping to weigh the need for them. As a result, I sense that the family is beginning to tune me out.

To them, my commands seem as inevitable as the sunrise.

Show me how to be silent, God.

It seems so ironic that I, who so admire a well-modulated voice, have sharpened into a strident and opinionated busybody. That's a harsh description—but an accurate one.

Wipe your feet. Say "please." Button your coat.

Once in a while, I need to give one of the children a reminder.

Once in a while. That's the key.

The rest of the time, please still my tongue. Let me wait to see what they can remember by themselves.

Thank you.

"I Can Do It Myself"

It's the Age of Independence, God.

My small son squats on the pavement, laboriously trying to tie his shoes.

I offer to help, but,

"No." He fights with the shoelace and his stubby fingers and his pride. "No. I can do it myself."

How many times a day does a mother hear that?

I can do it myself. I can do it myself. These children try and try and almost always fail in the end, coming to me for help as a last recourse.

Oh God, the things they think they can accomplish! They know . . . they just *know* . . . they can pour drinks of water, draw their own baths, make their own beds . . .

And I have to let them try. It's time they tested their wings, though I want to weep each time they botch a job.

I can do it myself . . . Drifting off to sleep at night, I hear dream-echoes of those five words.

And I know, with bittersweet certainty, that in a brief time their dependence on me will have passed.

Soon they'll be flawlessly executing any job they set out to do.

Give me patience, God, as they struggle through these proud and independent years. Let me help them, just enough. Thank you.

Not in Public

It was a shopper's nightmare, God. Throngs of frantic, pushing people were snatching up sale merchandise, then elbowing to the crowded dressing rooms. The department store was hot, muggy, disorganized—a human pressure cooker.

As I shrank toward the exit, a harried mother spanked her child in the middle of an aisle. The harder she spanked, the louder the cries grew. Clusters of embarrassed people averted their eyes . . . or watched openly to see what would happen next.

I was never going to discipline a child in public.

A mantle of wisdom was going to settle round my shoulders when I became a mother, enabling me to handle store hysterics quietly, efficiently, and inconspicuously.

Then the babies were born, and grew up a bit . . . and sometimes they pitched an embarrassing fit in the middle of a shopping center.

What can a parent do, God? I looked at alternatives.

Then I spanked.

The last time it happened, I saw a young woman's face contort in distaste. Her eyes told me: *I'll never spank a child of mine in public.*

My eyes asked her: *How will you keep from it?*

Three Years Old Today

Happy birthday to you! Happy birthday to you!

It's his first party, God. He's having such a wonderful time.

For once he's sitting, kinglike, in the middle of a group of friends. Boys and girls who couldn't be troubled with him yesterday (when he was an inconsequential two) are jostling to get closer to him today (for he's three, and the birthday child).

He's blown wax candles out, splattering the chocolate cake with wet enthusiasm. Presents have been unwrapped; favors have been doled out.

How his face is glowing, God!

He is so buoyant and happy today—so proud of being three.

Strange, how time has slipped by. I can close my eyes and recapture visions of my own mother, presiding at children's parties two decades ago . . .

But today is *his* birthday.

Please give him years to grow on.

Our Turn

It looks like a tornado touch-down, Lord.

Toys are strewn everywhere. Shoes and socks stagger in a trail toward the bed. The furniture is tattooed with childish autographs, scrawled in indelible crayon.

Yesterday we had the neighborhood children in to play—all of them.

It was our turn. The lady down the street had entertained them two days in a row. So, largely out of a sense of guilt, I declared Reciprocation Day.

For six hours, boys and girls and toddlers of uncertain sex wandered in and out of the nursery. I supervised them for the first part of the day, then grew irritable and snappish, and withdrew to the kitchen.

And in the time I was gone, all this plundering and pillaging took place.

As I kneel against the mess those children created, I am aghast. Please stem this tide of anger and resentment, Lord. If I'd been with them, doing my job, none of this would have happened.

In any event, yesterday gave me an education of sorts. I asked my neighbor how *she* managed the toddler hordes; what ground rules she imposed on them.

"None," she told me, smiling. "I don't see or hear them. They play in the back yard."

Isn't she wise, God?

Hungry

They're so terribly hungry, God.

Twenty minutes after dinner, they're begging for something more to nibble on. Fruit. Candy. A piece of chicken. *Anything.*

They're reed-thin, so I can't refuse them on grounds of too-many-calories.

There are other considerations, however.

My grocery bill has almost doubled this year. I don't know how much longer I can afford to play the part of mother bountiful.

Bless me with good humor as I wait at the market check-out stand, watching our food bill grow and grow.

Help me to remember that these bags of groceries will fire my children with energy, replenish their brain cells, and keep them alert and productive.

I'm aghast at the cost of food, and about how quickly it vanishes.

I'm grateful, though, that we are able to nourish our family adequately.

And I offer a special prayer for your children who endure far worse than this.

Sam the Bear

Thank you, God, for my little boy's Teddy bear.

Sam the Bear is ragged and torn and one of his button eyes is dangling by a thread.

None of that matters to my son, however.

From time immemorial, Sam the Bear has been a good-luck talisman.

When it's dark outside, Sam and his magic powers keep my son's fears at bay. When it's lonely, a hug from Sam is soothing and reassuring. When it's rainy and boring, Sam sheds his bear-identity and becomes a pirate, an astronaut, a daddy, or a much-needed friend.

Nothing touches me quite so much as the vision of Sam and my little boy, locked together in sleep, a warm, pink arm slung over a fuzzy, brown one.

I know, God—I *know*—that Sam is just a toy, but he has been so faithful and loving I wish I had the power to give him life, sometimes.

Wouldn't it be wonderful if each of us could have a sturdy, undemanding friend like Sam?

Life and Art

I'm looking at a family portrait my three-year-old sketched this afternoon. The Daddy and Mommy have huge heads and enormous eyes. Our arms are as long as the Amazon River, yet we teeter on tiny, twiglike legs, from which outsized feet balloon. At our elephantine feet, two dwarflike children cower, holding hands.

Is that how my child sees himself, God? As an insignificant gnat, hardly larger than my feet? Is that how my husband and I look to him? Are we such all-seeing, all-knowing, all-threatening giants?

For a moment I tremble, wondering if I can locate my old child psychology texts and do an amateur analysis on this disturbing picture.

Then I feel a jolt of gladness—for I notice that the two giants are smiling. Huge, Bunyanesque smiles, God. My husband's grin collides with his drooping purple moustache, but he looks benevolent, for all that.

As long as I must look like a giant to my babies, please let me look like a friendly, approachable giant. Let me smile a lot. Let me reach out and touch them with my huge, loving hands. Let me encircle their vulnerable bodies with my Popeye-sized arms. I love them so, God. Don't let me intimidate or frighten them. Please.

Read Me a Story

It happened again today, God, and I'm so ashamed.

My little girl crept up behind me, storybook in hand, with a wide, expectant smile crinkling her lips and lighting her eyes.

"Read me a story, Mom," she begged me, holding out a dog-eared book. "Read me a story . . . please?"

"Sure," I told her. "Later on, okay?" Then I went ahead with furniture-polishing, or dishwashing, or letter-writing, or whatever it was that seemed so important at the time.

She waited patiently for a while, clutching her book and trying to decipher the strange words with her untutored eyes. Then she sighed and abandoned the slim volume (what a short time it would have taken to read it!), dejectedly looking elsewhere for something to do.

The book was never read.

It's tucked back on the shelf now—its story still a mystery to my sleeping child.

I'm so sorry about what happened today. I wish I could wake my daughter and read to her now, but she's slumbering peacefully, a snoring, oblivious mass of curls.

A few more hours and it will be morning, God.

Won't you remind me to read to her then?

The Accident

It was an old cup, Lord. The filigree had faded and grown brittle with the passing of years. Like many heirlooms, it was valuble only because we loved it.

Now my daughter has shattered it. Its delicate porcelain lies on the floor, a pathetic heap of splinters and shards.

I'm quivering with anger. It doesn't make sense, I know, to mourn the passing of a material thing. Still, the hurt is there. I want to strike out, to hit somebody, to somehow vent this mounting rage.

"How could you?" I shout at my little girl. Her stricken face avoids mine. "How could you be so clumsy? I loved that cup! You *knew* I loved it!"

Help me to stop a minute, to rearrange my priorities.

Help me, Lord, to get past "things." Let the acquisition of them not matter so terribly. Let me remain blind to their rarity, their beauty, their cost.

They are nothing, really.

They are nothing at all—compared to this grieving child.

Welcome Home

They're best friends, Lord.

The two of them hang around together and fight like sisters. About half the time, they're furious with each other.

When summer came, Jenny departed on a week-long trip to the mountains. While she was gone, my little girl played listlessly, flipping through much-read books and aimlessly coloring pictures. She watched too many cartoons and teased her brother and asked for half-a-dozen snacks a day.

The hours crawled.

Toward the end of the week, every time she heard a car door slam, she thought it was Jenny's car. Every time the doorbell rang, she hoped it would be Jenny standing on the front porch . . .

Finally, Jenny's family motored in, tired and almost ill from their marathon drive. All they wanted in the world, I'm sure, was *no company.*

But the two girls spotted each other, and raced, squealing with pleasure, into each other's arms. Then they strolled off to Jenny's back yard, to play on the swing set.

God, please bless their beautiful, mercurial friendship. They can't live with each other . . . but they *certainly* can't live without each other, as they discovered this week.

Cut from the Team

Please bless and cheer this little boy, Lord.

He's been thrown out of a neighborhood ball game. And though he gruffly muttered that it "doesn't matter," he disappeared into his room. I hear quiet sobbing behind his door; the dejected *thump-bump* of his ball hitting the floor.

He has so many gifts, God, and I thank you for them. But athletic prowess isn't one of them.

He simply lacks the natural grace and facility to manipulate a football or baseball. His swimming lessons are going only moderately well. He runs unevenly and awkwardly.

Yet how he tries!

I watch him in quiet anguish, God. His mind is excellent. He handles himself well in groups of people. I think he's going to grow into a fine man some day.

But I *don't* think he's going to be first-string varsity athlete. And that, above all other things, is what he wants.

I want him to develop his body as best he can. I want it to be healthy and trim and efficient, equal to his needs.

But I know him so well. And I know his limitations. Please help me to show him that the world is more than a football game.

Mary and Martha

One woman I know is a natural parent. She's a real earth mother . . . full of warmth and patience and granola recipes. Sometimes it seems as if she wanders about in a cloud of love for children and home and domestic duties.

How does she do it, God?

We have the same number of children. We have the same money problems. The same frightening set of responsibilities.

Yet she's serenity personified. Her house and her children are always clean. She's perpetually creased and made up and combed out.

Oh, God. She's a good friend. I love her—but I can't emulate her. Her tidiness and calm acceptance of household crises confound me. Her organization leaves me aghast at my own haphazard life-style.

I don't envy her, God. I prefer my own children, my own husband, my own house—unkempt though they may be—to hers. Yet I always have to fight a sort of wistfulness, after visiting with this friend, this perfect mother, this uncomplaining wife. I always feel I have to justify my own imperfections after a coffee klatch in her glistening kitchen.

God, I like to think of the two of us as Mary and Martha, sometimes. I like to remember that both of those blessed women served you, each in her own way—and that you accepted and appreciated the offerings of each.

If I can't be the housekeeper she is—and I can't, I tried once in a spurt of energy—help me to develop the redeeming features remaining to me. Help me to value my own gifts, even if they're not immediately apparent to others. Thank you, God.

In Sickness

It's late, and I've been taking care of this sick little boy all day. My eyes are burning and my mind is numb. I crave sleep, but I'm afraid to close my eyes while his fever is so high; while the chills are so hard.

God, stay close to me tonight. Freshen me, so I can remember what symptoms to watch for, what medicines to administer. And keep me from getting sick myself, for I'm holding the family together now. I need to stay vigorous and well.

Tonight I marvel at the power a mother has to soothe and comfort. Until the medicine does its work, I can calm my son by holding his hand, brushing his damp hair behind his ears, and placing a cool cloth on his forehead.

I don't know why any of those things help, but they seem to. As mothers have done for hundreds of years, I pour love out to my sick child. This, too, is a medicine; perhaps the most effective of all.

As disturbing as a child's illness is, there is a pleasant sense of closeness between us tonight, and I am uplifted by it, God. I will some of my strength, my energy into this small, distressed body. Take what you can from me, God, and give it to this little one. Please restore him to health as quickly as possible.

Do You Like Me?

Do you like me?
No, I love you.
My daughter has a need, God.

She needs to be reassured of her importance. She needs to be held and cherished. She needs great chunks of time lavished on her, but most important,

She needs to be liked.

At this juncture in her life, *like* is more important than *love*. *Like* is earned, not inherited . . . and she understands this even now.

I shall always love her, and she knows it, so she's gone on to the next plateau of caring—

Do you like me?

The next time she poses that question, God, let me not equivocate about family bonds and degrees of affection. Rather, let me look squarely and directly into her yearning eyes.

Let me answer, in the simple monosyllable she craves,

Yes.

How About a New Baby?

There's a new baby in the neighborhood. The children are enchanted—and green with envy.

It's all well and good to *visit* a baby, they tell me. But it's not like having your very own baby at home.

I know.

And I know something else. These two are beginning an organized campaign.

When they decide jointly that they want something, they're unmerciful in their pursuit of it . . . bicycles, babies, puppies, plastic swimming pools.

Beginning today, they'll take turns assaulting my tired ears with pleas for a baby—their whim of the moment.

They'll promise to accept no gifts for the holidays . . . if only they can have a baby. They'll vow to take care of it themselves (like the cat). They'll don their longest faces when I tell them "no."

This would be rather amusing, God, if it weren't so annoying. There's nothing in the world quite as exasperating as demanding, cajoling children.

Awaken them, please, to the bounty of their home —the pleasures that already exist here. Teach them to be content. Let them discipline their desires, and contain their whims.

They Grow So Fast

They are growing up so fast, God.

Yesterday, I was in a frenzy of impatience to rush them through a particularly troublesome age.

Now, their bodies are racing toward adulthood, developing almost too quickly.

And as they spurt upwards physically, emotional changes are taking place, too.

Not long ago, I could hold them tightly against me, and they snuggled as contentedly as a pair of puppies. We nuzzled and tickled and rolled on the floor together, their shrill gut-giggling making raucous echoes throughout the house.

Nowadays, they prefer to maintain a more dignified distance. Once in a while, when they're in a particularly generous mood, they'll let me kiss them or hug them.

Those moments are rare, though, God.

When these children irritate, procrastinate, aggravate—please reawaken me to the passage of time.

Roger

One morning he just appeared for breakfast, God. He was dirty and scruffy, about four years old. As I spooned hot cereal into the children's bowls, he looked on longingly.

"Would you like some?" I asked him.

So he stayed to share our meal. I found out from other mothers in the neighborhood that he breakfasts with them, too. When he senses that he's overstayed his welcome, he moves on to another house.

What should we do about Roger? Both his parents are gone all day. They don't know where he is most of the time. Perhaps they don't even care.

Clearly, this is none of my business. But he's little more than a baby, God.

He breaks my heart.

Show me how to help. Please.

The Snake Pit

They have this kids-only secret club, God.

No mothers allowed—they're very sorry, but that means *no* mothers.

The club meets in the Snake Pit, a harmless wooded hollow that is neither a pit nor snake-infested.

As far as I can tell, about all the Snake Pit Gang does is smuggle peanut butter sandwiches into meetings. After a conclave, there are sandwich scraps and cardboard boxes and story books scattered around. It looks harmless enough.

Please bestow your blessings on the Snake Pit Gang, God. Fire their young imaginations with wondrous adventures. Let them have all the fun they can in the Pit, now, while they're this once-in-a-lifetime magic age.

Give them small mysteries to solve and riddles to riddle. Keep the big shade tree they play beneath richly dressed with cooling leaves.

And when their club is disbanded and the Snake Pit lies deserted, please let their memories of this happy, irresponsible time warm and comfort them.

Pray Without Ceasing

My daughter just discovered prayer, God—and I can't turn her off.

If your earthly petitions seem dominated of late by a young girl's recitations, they probably came from this house.

She has taken to praying with such zeal that she makes the rest of the family ashamed.

Before we dare eat, we're admonished to "say the bless-its." Before we slip under the covers for the night, a piping voice calls out, "Wait! We forgot to do 'Now I lay me . . .' "

It may be out of the ordinary to thank you for prayer, but I am grateful—particularly for the prayers of children.

In their enthusiasm for spiritual communion, they freshen us. The worn-out rituals we murmur each week somehow breathe again, with new meaning, when they're recited by a child.

When my daughter prays, she knows she's speaking directly to you. She doesn't mess around with metaphysical notions of an abstract divinity. She *believes*.

Thank you for the friendship you've shared with this little girl; thank you for letting me be privy to the secrets of her uncomplicated soul.

It's so wonderful when you're a child, God.

Four—and Holding

His nose is pressed against the window.

Everyone in the neighborhood is off to school, it seems—everyone except him.

Disconsolate, he shoves his hands in his pockets and kicks his way toward his sister's room. Within minutes, he's turned it into a junk pile—and tried to provoke a hair-pulling match with her.

"Am I in trouble?" he challenges me, as I survey the destruction. "Are you gonna spank me?"

Suddenly this scruffy, mischievous four-year-old is embarrassingly transparent.

"Being in trouble" is better than being ignored.

A spanking, dreaded by both of us, will at least reaffirm his importance; his ability to upset routine.

God, please help him to get through this difficult period as gracefully as possible.

He's just an overripe preschooler, ready to have a life away from home, but not legally eligible to attend class.

We're stuck with each other for the academic year.

Won't you help him to like himself better, for the next few months?

Move Slowly, with Caution

I nearly killed a child today, God.

As I was backing the car out of our drive, I heard a harsh, sickening crunch—then the most frightening silence I have ever known.

Trembling, I braced myself to inspect the damage.

A neighbor child's tricycle had been smashed beyond repair. In haste, I had forgotten to check for toys and children behind the car.

Thank you, God, for teaching me a lesson cheaply. A tricycle can be replaced—but not the child who rides it.

Thank you, thank you, for sparing that child.

As I rush through your gift of days, please remind me that lives can be lost through haste and carelessness.

Please help me to protect your smallest children, until they can, themselves, learn caution.

The Money Problem

God, I don't know what to do.

I'm facing a stack of bills, and I don't have enough money to pay them all.

I don't even have enough to keep all our creditors happy.

There's a sick, sinking sensation in my stomach. Our family has doubled in size, and our income is halved.

Even if I went back to work, I don't think we could pull out of this financial quagmire. There would be a baby-sitter to pay, and carfare, and a basic working wardrobe to buy.

Our financial plans were well laid, God. We haven't bought needless luxuries. But there have been sicknesses with the children. Our car wouldn't start. The roof began to leak. The washing machine broke down.

I don't feel we're less fortunate than surrounding families. Everyone I know has emergency expenses.

Everyone I know is concerned about money . . .

Please reassure my husband that things will get better someday. He's eaten up with worry. Please let this household run smoothly for a time, until we can honor our obligations.

Thank you.

Storm Clouds on the Horizon

God, teach us to be gentle with each other.

Today we've been unsettled. We've taken on more responsibilities than we can handle, and now we're left to deal with the troublesome residue of deadlines and pressures.

It would be so easy to lash out at each other in front of the children . . . or to lash out *at* the children. Right now, we're maintaining a harsh silence that could ruin the rest of this day.

I'm really ready to spar this morning; to raise my voice and cut down anyone unlucky enough to be in my path.

Please help me to rein in these turbulent emotions. Or if I must explode for the sake of my physical or mental health, then help me to choose an inanimate "opponent" —give me the sense to wallop a pillow instead of a child.

Oh, God, what a lousy day. What a waste. Why do we allow ourselves to be swallowed up by external demands? I'm in the mood to shut the door of my house and withdraw for a while.

Help me to turn disaster-time around, won't you? We could salvage the afternoon, at least, if we started right now.

Dark Outside

It's dark and rainy outside, God. A delicious night to curl under the blankets . . . I can hardly keep my eyes open.

As I'm drifting off, I hear a small child whimpering down the hall.

Maybe he'll go back to sleep . . .

But the whimper grows in intensity, becoming a lusty cry.

It's no use, God. Somehow I have to wake up, throw on a robe, and grope through the dark house to the nursery.

Once I'm there, a tiny, nightgowned figure hiccups in relief.

"Mommy! Mom! I'm afraid of the dark! I'm afraid!" So I reach out for the sobbing bundle of nightgown-and-baby, and try to hug its fears away.

Why are children so afraid of the dark?

Night is so gentle and peaceful. The sounds of evening are such welcome benedictions to our harried days.

What phantoms do children see, through their young and impressionable eyes? What menacing noises do they imagine?

I'm so drowsy right now all I want to do is crawl into bed and close my eyes . . . but this child is stiff with terror, keenly attuned to my every move.

How can I soothe him, God?

My Love, My Television

Look at them, God: slumped on the couch, mesmerized by a flickering television set. They'll watch anything that moves.

And look at me: I'm letting it happen.

Some women crave an afternoon cigarette—I crave Cartoon Carnival.

It's a vapid program, but it amuses them. If I turn on cartoons, it means two hours of peace and quiet for me . . . two hours of perfect obedience from them.

God, I know this is wrong.

I know I should be reading to them, talking to them, taking them for walks.

But when I reach for the "off" button, it's so easy to rationalize: *today was tiring, it won't hurt them, I need the time alone . . .*

What do you want me to do, God? Tell me.

How do I kick their five-show-a-day habit? Show me.

This must sound terribly unimportant to you. But television—*television!*—has turned out to be the strongest temptation yet.

Kindergarten

It was going to be Freedom Year, God.

Kindergarten! Four glorious hours of it, five times a week!

Oh, I had plans for those hours. Reading. Sewing. Shopping. Relaxing. Whipping the house into shape, and having it remain clean and untouched the rest of the day.

I was going to learn how to be an adult again. Years of confinement with small children had diminished my vocabulary; "mommified" my personality.

Four hours a day . . . it was going to make all the difference.

Then kindergarten actually started. And I discovered that room-mothering, chaperoning, and fund-raising were going to occupy a considerable amount of my "free" time.

That's all right, God.

The kindergarten teacher is overworked, underpaid, and desperate for help. I really don't mind pitching in.

I wonder, though . . .

Next term, could they have some craft weeks? Some partyless weeks? Some weeks without field trips?

(Weeks without me?)

Thank you.

Kids and Pets

Is that cat friendly? they asked.

The cat became Friendly that day, and you know the rest of the story, God.

Friendly the Cat gave them something to love, something to be bigger than, and something to care for.

They drug her around and dressed her up.

They fed her and brushed her and sneaked her into their rooms at night. They tried to make her purr, and smuggled food scraps under the table.

Look, Friendly's softing me! They even coined new words to describe her antics.

When no one else in the world is friendly, Friendly has comforted them.

Bless this special bond, God.

Payoff Time

It must be time for the payoff, Lord.

I can't put my finger on exactly when things eased up. But they have.

All that diligent scolding and hugging and kissing must have "taken," because the children are behaving in an exemplary fashion.

They've been helping to clean their rooms. They've tried to set the evening table for me. They've had only one argument in the last week, and that was a mild one, quickly resolved.

Several people have commented lately on what good children they are. My usual reaction has been to laugh shortly and say, "You should see them at home."

That's unjust, God. Because they *are* good. I'm really proud of them. As lively and inventive and energetic as they are, I know this sterling behavior doesn't come naturally.

I sense that they're really struggling to behave. It's been a comfortable, peaceful time for all of us; a healing time.

Soon enough, we'll be in the throes of battle again. They're still at such competitive, combative ages.

The respite has been wonderful, though.

Thank you, God.

Babies Come from *There?*

They want to know where babies come from, God.
I guess it's time to tell them.

Sex has always been joyous and matter-of-fact in our marriage, so I'm not really afraid of having this talk with them.

Besides, they're level-headed children. I think they can absorb whatever information I give them in their commonsensical way.

Yet I'm still uneasy.

I want, so much, to impress upon them how love and sex are interdependent.

I want them to have some concept of how the consummation of love is far, far more than some strange gratification rite.

Work with me, God. Help me to paint a comfortable, reassuring, and natural picture of sex for them. Keep me from mincing words. But keep me, too, from acting too detached and coldly objective about one of the warmest, loveliest parts of life.

They're waiting, God.
Here we go.

Does It Hurt to Die?

I thought I had sated their curiosity about death, God. We've talked about heaven and Jesus and being so old and tired that death is a sweet relief.

But they had more questions today. And I'm so afraid I handled things badly . . . muddled answers, or sounded unsure of myself.

"Does it hurt to die?" they asked me. "If you go to heaven, how do you *know* it's going to be a good place?"

Then, "We don't *want* to die. Do we *have* to die?"

They were very subdued and disturbed this afternoon. Tonight they both had nightmares . . . about dying.

Oh, God. Help me! I've had many tests of faith, but I think this is the hardest one you've sent my way.

It's hard because, though I know you and love you with all of my heart, I can't chart geographic boundaries of heaven. I can't give a description of the place.

Their questions are so anxious, Lord. Their need for comfort and reassurance is so urgent.

Please make me equal to their needs. Please give me the gift of trust, so I can transmit it to them.

Thank you.

I Dressed Myself

You should have seen her, Lord.

My daughter bounded into the kitchen this morning, all arms and legs and excitement.

"Look!" she said, beaming. "I dressed myself!"

I looked . . . and she certainly *had*.

She wore a tattered wool skirt, a blazing tangerine bathing suit top, and a snow hat.

And she was so proud; so very excited.

From the looks of her, she must have dug through half-a-dozen drawers and charity bags to find that bizarre combination. She had struggled with buttons and zippers and a chin-strap, before emerging, gloriously colorful, a mismatched Monarch butterfly . . .

What would you have said, Lord, if you had been here—and were expected to respond to that spectacle?

It was such a terrible outfit—and so lovingly selected.

I looked at her for a long space of minutes as she did an impatient dance in (I hadn't seen those before) her rabbit-ear bedroom slippers.

Then I relented. Her smile was too expectant.

"You're beautiful," I said.

Emergency

We're having a household emergency, God. Please help me.

I have to check into a hospital. Right now—not later.

My husband is away on business. So it's just the sympathetic physician, and me, and the children.

I hurt like crazy, but through the pain, I'm reminded of so many things I have to do . . .

Find my husband. Get a message to him, somehow.

Locate someone who will take care of our children for an indefinite period of time. Drive them to wherever they'll be staying . . .

Pack my clothes.

Secure the house.

And the pain is growing, growing . . .

This is a prayer for efficiency. Please let me function with unclouded judgment until these important chores are taken care of. Help me to hide my panic from my son and daughter.

Teach me to be tough, God. On this difficult day, let me be rational, not emotional. Let me make the right decisions, quickly.

Thank you.

Hmmm

"Don't do that, what you're doing."

I put the newspaper down and stared at my daughter. "All right," I said. "Sure. What was I doing?"

She shot me her disgusted look, that cross between a sneer and a grimace. *"You* know," she said meaningfully. "You were going *hmmm.* You always go *hmmmm."*

Do I, God?

I mean to listen to my children when they talk, but they never really *quit* talking. Or if one does quit, the other starts up immediately.

I mean to answer their questions thoughtfully, in complete sentences. I mean to look them straight-in-the-eye when they ask me something.

But somewhere along the line, I just chucked it all and hid behind a newspaper. If there's an emergency, I come out. Otherwise, no.

Our conversations are pretty laughable, I suppose. They say "mumble mumble." And I respond with a well-considered, "hmmm." That's terse, but it's a signal that I'm breathing, that I love them, that I need to be alone.

Is it time to sublimate my need, and consider theirs?
What do you think, Lord?

"Will He Give Me a Shot Today?"

He's a squaller and a bawler, God.

Right now, he's huddled against the doctor's table, waiting for some forgotten inoculation. Behind his stricken face, a cow is jumping over the moon.

"This won't hurt a bit," his nurse murmurs . . . then jabs.

And despite his thrashing legs and embarrassing cries, I thank you for the protection he is about to receive.

Bless this vaccine as it courses through his young body, eliminating one dread disease from his future.

I'm indebted to the scientist who discovered it, and grateful to you for allowing my child to enjoy its benefits.

Please let him reach manhood in glowing good health, God.

Thank you.

Moving Day

This is what remains of our life here, God: a sagging pyramid of cardboard boxes, stacked in back of a moving van.

We're leaving this house; this neighborhood.

Somewhere far away are friends we haven't met— a home we've never seen.

It was exciting for a time. We convinced each other that we were ready for a larger house; a fresh beginning.

But today's the day. And suddenly I'm chilled at the prospect of leaving this beloved community.

Moving seems so irrevocable now. So *forever.*

The children huddle together, lost in their own thoughts and secret apprehensions. It's going to be a difficult adjustment for them.

Please, God, let this be the right step for us to take.

Bless our new home, and warm the old one for its future tenants.

Training Wheels

God, please watch over these children as they attempt to master the intricacies of the bicycle.

Ever since their two glistening racers were purchased, our bathroom has doubled as a first-aid station. Knees have been skinned, elbows have been purpled—but nothing discourages the intrepid riders.

Please keep my children on a firm, smooth course. Let small mistakes of balance be forgiven, as they jolt over chuckholes and pitted sidewalks.

Allow, if you can, a few days of grace for old wounds to heal, before new, even angrier bruises appear.

Thank you for their perseverance.

Thank you, too, for their courage; for the keen sense of fun they derive from this new sport.

Let them cultivate an unwavering sense of balance, God—in cycling, and in life.

L-M-N-O-P

First-grade teachers are pretty serious about this, God.

They send home an official-looking directive that says: *a well-prepared child will begin class knowing his alphabet.*

I hadn't thought my children were ill-prepared . . . but perhaps they are.

Both of them can zip through the alphabet, until they reach "L." Then, a hoarse garble that sounds like "eluhmenopee" results.

We have struggled valiantly to separate those five wicked letters, to no avail. I've gotten small mirrors for them to place in front of their mouths.

"Watch," I have said, in quiet desperation. "Llllllllll."

"Llllll," they repeat dutifully, wiggling their tongues.

Still, when the time comes to put the whole thing together, from A to Z, they bog down in "eluhmenopee" again.

Help me, oh God, resolve the problem of "eluhmenopee" before September.

Please.

We want them to be "well-prepared," don't we?

First Day of School

I couldn't wait, God.

When school opened, I knew there would be so many pleasures for my child . . . so much free time for me.

Today was the first day.

And suddenly, my eldest—who has looked so gawky, so mature, so absolutely *ripe* for school—seemed dwarfed by his regulation-size lunch box.

We made an elaborate ceremony of No Breakfast, and contemplated the awesome morning ahead.

With great seriousness, our new first grader insisted that I:

not kiss him at school.

not talk to his teacher.

not be late at day's end.

not cry.

Four orders, God! He must have been formulating them throughout an apprehensive night.

Please help me to calm this anxious child.

Watch over him, just until he gets the hang of things.

Thank you.

Where Did They Come From?

Where did they come from, God?

They are so straight and tall and beautiful.

Their souls are so clean and unsullied.

Their hearts are so uncomplicated by hatred, resentment, fear.

When I look at my husband, their father, I see a tall, handsome man, with an ineffably kind face and merry gray eyes.

When I look in a mirror, searching for myself, I see straight brown hair, blue eyes, a sprinkling of freckles . . . the mask of a contented woman.

What a beautiful marriage we have, God! Like all other men and women, we've fallen in and out of love, in and out of happiness . . . but in the end, we always come together, closer than before.

We belong together, God. I guess we always will.

And from our union, these children came, squalling and slick and red and unshaped.

Now they're blooming, God. The genes we provided are there, still. But they are becoming less of us each day, I think. More of themselves. And more of you.

Just look at them, God—you must have had a hand in shaping them.

They're such special children. I love them so much.

Thank you.

The Guilty Party

I've been whipping myself again, God.

Every time something misfires in this family, I feel guilt.

When a baby becomes sick, I examine my actions for the previous week. Was a coat left unbuttoned? Were the meals unbalanced? Was outside play allowed on a frosty day?

I'm to blame!

If my husband becomes moody, I feel he's reacting to me. Have I burdened him with too many complaints? Have I fretted about finances? Have I bored him with too much household chatter?

I caused his problem!

What quirk is there in me, and in most of the mothers I know, that attracts responsibility for all the difficulties our families encounter?

Help me, God. Let me abandon this egocentric guilt. Let me assume responsibility for my own life, and for the safety of my children.

Then let me relax.

Show me how to spread the responsibilities and concerns around. Please.

The Pleasure of My Company Is Requested

God, I feel so awkward and ugly tonight.

We're getting ready for a party. I'm dressed in refurbished velvet and someone else's jewels.

Staring at me from the mirror is a woman with light rings of makeup around the eyes, to mask the tiredness. Her hand-me-down dress hangs badly on the sturdy, work-worn frame. The hair is bristling with static. Too clean. Or too dry. Too *something*.

There was a time when appearances didn't matter to me. I was proud of the woman inside this body—meeting the public wasn't frightening, then.

It's almost more than I can bear, now.

Tonight I'm going to have to try to project myself out of budget problems, worries about the children, and lethargy.

I have to come alive. I have to make conversation.

Somehow, please God, I have to make my husband proud.

My Love Is a River

My love is a river, God. It flows easily and naturally, even as it meets obstacles and sudden pitfalls. Like rain in a river, my sorrows, my tears, serve to intensify that love —to toughen and strengthen it.

Like a river, my love seemingly abates and rebuilds with the season—but it never really diminishes. It never really runs dry.

When my heart is sore and anxious—when I am afraid—my love is like a peaceful, healing river, soothing the parched landscape as it winds and twists through its ancient bed.

When the children are irascible and testy, when my inadequacies as a mother frighten me, then my love goes the way of a faithful river, buoying me up and greening me with confidence and reinforcing my dwindling reserves of strength.

When I am physically tired and drained, then the river of my love carries me through the completion of tasks I must perform for these vulnerable young ones, the children.

This shell of a body is sadly frail and limited sometimes, and the demands on it are great.

So happily I transcend the fatigue, the discomfort, and the limitations. I turn inward, to the river of my love, and like an endless spring, my love carries me on and on.